BEAUTY UN

BEAUTY UNSUSPECTED

Athena Stevens

ISBN 978-1-291-04350-1

This book was typeset in Stempel Garamond by *Steve Lambley Information Design*, The Hague. It was edited by Dr. J. Gill Holland.

Front cover image taken by Will Hutchinson at Greenland Dock.

This book was inspired through the actions and input of countless others.

*To the Pirates of Greenland Dock, who always show me wisdom,
beauty, and grace where few would suspect their presence.*

And to Jason, who taught me to recognise these things in the first place.

Contents

Introduction

I became a writer at the age of three when my parents bought me a small blank book for my birthday. My father agreed to take dictation for me every night so that I could keep a journal, as I was unable to write myself. What a three year old could find to journal about was an entirely different matter altogether. However, at a very young age I was instilled with the idea that I could write, and it was a worthwhile use of my time.

Within about a year, my acting career also began, again, with the help of my parents. My mother would work weekends as a visiting nurse while trying to make ends meet, and spend as much time with her child as so many young parents strive to do. Therefore, during Saturday and Sunday I spent time with my father each weekend creating a theatrical production to greet my mother when she returned home, exhausted, on Sunday evening. Often my father would agree to play narrator or hold a flashlight as a spot in order to make the production seem that much more worthy of my mother's artistic praise.

In my mind, acting and writing have always been taken for granted as what were supposed to be the vocations of my life. Even during my days of adolescence and early adulthood, when I assumed that a professional acting career was out of the question owing to my disability, and I opted for the sturdier career path of law, it always felt as if I were put on this earth for creative expression—and for the ability to put ideas into other people's minds. Any other career path felt like wearing a hand-me-down dress.

To commit yourself to being a professional actor, while still having a disability, is to willingly take on the obstacles and shackles of society. People were disappointed, I have now been told, when I went away to college and decided to major in theatre rather than devoting myself strictly to a more academic pursuit. Ironically, I suppose, both those people and I myself missed the point of a liberal arts education. In that sort of college setup, you learn and study for the sake of learning, not necessarily for a vocational trade. But still, in my early twenties, I would explain to individuals that I wished to be an actress and they would reply "Do you really believe that is a realistic possibility?" Perhaps not, but without the attempt by individuals to beat the odds, society never progresses.

Writing, on the other hand, has exactly the opposite effect. I am not inhibited by my body, my speech, or my reaction time. I can write as swiftly and as well as anyone else. It is in writing that I am able to throw off the manacles that I willingly take on as an actor and explore ideas to a depth and breadth that is unrestricted and goes as far as my imagination can take me. It is in writing that I am completely able-bodied, and thus can operate at as full capacity as anyone regardless of physical limitations.

I suppose it is because I knew I had this freedom and privilege with a blank page that I spent so many of my educational years focused on acting. If I was clearly at a disadvantage in this corner of my pursuits, it made sense that acting is what I needed to focus on in order to make my dreams a reality. After my first play premiered in Covent Garden last year, I was reminded that I was a writer as well as the performer who worked so hard all these years.

This book represents a collection of personal narratives, essays, and reflections that I have written after moving to London. Indeed, this is the only city where I have ever been a fully functioning adult. In many ways, it's become the best home I could possibly have imagined as that small girl sitting beside my father at bedtime writing notes about her day. In other ways I am still very much a stranger in a strange land. I choose to both live in London and be an actor despite the fact that it is a lifestyle which is still massively inaccessible and even hostile towards individuals living with disabilities. While living this way I must accept these elements of inaccessibility and socially imposed obstacles which are not of my own making. I could choose to live in a small town where I can get into every shop, and all the people I meet are aware of my needs and difficulties. I could choose to only be a writer or something entirely more financially stable. But avoiding social adversity has never been conducive to creativity, and it is not without both adversity and conflict that we understand what it is to be human. Set before me in this life are two tasks: the expansion of Imagination and the restoration of dignity to the Human Condition.

Much of my time spent in London has been about recognising we live in an inaccessible and unjust world and then learning how to navigate my way around these barriers and progress beyond them. Readers will note that this book has an ongoing "coming of age" theme. Indeed it should. If we are careful people, we get to spend our entire lives learning about this world and what our role is in it. If we are observant people, we see the imperfections of our world and refuse to become numb to its desperate needs. And if we are fortunate people, we will spend our entire lives growing into what we dreamed we'd become and finding that despite the numerous times we suspect otherwise, there is beauty everywhere in this life.

Athena Stevens
2 August 2012

GRACE NOTES

THE MAN STEPPED OUT OF THE SHADOWS of the rainy night like a snake lurking after its prey. Walking square into my path I swerved left, clearly not wanting to make conversation. *Please, just let me go home, I thought. I'm in no mood to deal with crazies tonight.*

"Excuse me, Miss. Do you like the opera?" Realising that we were standing in front of the opera house, I thought fast.

"Don't know. Never been. Good night," I quickly replied, trying anything to shut the conversation down. If there is one thing worse than talking to a crazy, it's talking to a semi-cultured crazy who is vaguely aware of his own surroundings.

"Would you like to go tonight?" The openness of the question took me by surprise. I had never been approached by someone scalping tickets before. Was that all there was to it? Just a simple proposition on the street corner? My parents live in Las Vegas, so the fact I was suspicious about any street proposal was not so much saying anything about the man now making a proposition outside the English National Opera House as it did about myself and subsequent background. "Look, Miss," he said, noticing my skepticism, "the ticket is right here. Check it for yourself."

From a tattered coat pocket he produced a single ticket with the ENO's official logo on it for that evening's performance of *Radimisto.* It had sold for ninety pounds.

"Don't you want it?" I began, stumbling for speech and trying to wrap my head around what was happening. I was being offered a ticket for

1

the best seat in the house to the opera, by a man who sold the *Big Issue* on the street.

"Nah, it's a warm night for November. I've seen this production about five times and I'm getting tired of it. Besides, you always smile at me when you go by and I like to see you smile. You've never been to the opera before, you said." Did I really smile at him? Usually, when I was going up that street I was in such a rush that I didn't think I noticed anybody.

"No, I've never been to the opera. I—I've always wanted to: but … I can't take this ticket, it's not for accessible seating," I stammered. Absolutely nothing in my life had remotely prepared me for a situation as gracious as this.

"Oh, that's not a problem. I know everyone on staff here. Eddie will change your ticket to one you can get to, no questions asked. I've known him for years. Let me just hide this *Big Issue* badge, so the public doesn't mind me, and we'll go in and I'll introduce you."

"I really don't deserve this," I muttered under my breath, realising my horrible actions of a few minutes ago.

"I've been to the opera over eighty times this year. I've been a drinker my whole life. I have failed people I love. Hurt them beyond repair. Look at me. Do you think, out of anyone in this city I deserve to go to the opera multiple times a week? People just give me their ticket when their friend can't make it or they have a conflict. I don't deserve it; it's a gift. It's grace." With that he took me inside.

After the performance that night, with the snow coming down against the taxi I took home, I had grace on my mind. It is one of the few words left in the English language that doesn't have a negative connotation. Charity, faith, hope, even love can be said in such a sneering tone that it gives the impression of naïveté and starry eyes. 'Grace' has yet to be soiled by such cynicism. There is no such thing, yet, as being too graceful. I have yet to read a performance review where the critic says, "The singer's grace was distracting and led to a loss of depth in the character." We love grace in all its forms, in movement, in character, in language, in passion. We talk about the 'grace of God' when we are afforded a fortune we do not deserve. We need grace; it binds us together when we should give up on failures, it takes our breath away and give us a reason to keep breathing in the same second, it shows the very best within us. In short, grace saves us from a very bleak existence.

I know that without being given grace myself, my life and all I have received in it would disappear. The amount of times I screw up in a single day constantly proves to me that I need to be showered with grace daily. Indeed, as Shakespeare wrote, "[I]n the course of justice, none of us should see salvation." But it is because I've been afforded grace by others, loved when I was unlovable, and given the best gifts in life when I did not deserve them, that I can pass on such grace to others. I am liberated by *Big Issue* salesmen on the street, the people who show me grace, and when all is said and done, I want to pass that freedom on to those who are held captive in an ungraceful world.

In music, a grace note is defined as "an extra note added as an embellishment and not essential to the harmony or melody." And perhaps in an aria or composition a grace note is not essential. In fact, many who do not find value in music or art may say the entire piece is inessential to life on this planet. We can survive without art, or music, or dance. But the fact that a Big Issue seller finds joy in being given tickets to the opera eighty times per year proves that we cannot survive without grace. The fact that he was willing to give his ticket to me, a cynical person more willing to rush about her day than look at the man right in front of her who offers a gift, proves it still further.

URBAN SLALOM

Sometimes I feel as if going through the streets of London is like being a footballer. Of course, that experience is not one that is unique on the field. Dodging couples trying to make out in the middle of the pathway or young mothers suddenly stopping to grab their children by the hand before they totter away can be equally as dangerous as trying to beat the clock for that last-minute goal.

London is considered by many to be the most civilised and, funny enough, the most advanced city in the world. And, looking at the city as a whole on a good day, this is largely true. You can top up your phone at any ATM, the trains run on time (as long as you fit into the ideal London body), you can go through your day relatively smoothly with your iPod in your ears and your purse in your hand, conducting business on the go, dropping into Fleet Street when necessary, and jumping on the train just before the door closes to make the most of time.

Oddly enough, with all this advancement and adaptation that is supposed to make life go as smooth as the silk of a new White House/ Black Market dress, we've lost something. As human beings in London, we have lost the entire skill of spatial awareness. The irony is, of course, westerners, particularly British westerners, in comparison to most cultures, feel the necessity of a relatively large amount of personal space. With this notion, one would assume, comes the ability to remain extremely well placed in the environment. Not so.

It would be easy for me to say that American tourists are the worst. And they are pretty bad—don't get me wrong. As an American myself, I often groan at the middle-aged woman in khaki shorts with her fanny pack with her flat drawl that can only come from Minnesota. She is in London to experience culture, and as such, she's doing her best to herd her children like a flock of geese. In doing so, of course, she is completely oblivious to those of us who still have a job while she is on vacation.

But it does not end with the tourists. It doesn't end with the individuals trying to get that perfect shot of Big Ben when they might just as easily hop into a local newspaper agent and get one ten times better. It doesn't stop with Regent's Park where the young people make out freely. It doesn't even stop in Covent Garden where the mixture of bipeds and motorists proves to be so deadly that no law can dare define the area. No, it doesn't stop there. Londoners will take their half out of the middle as much as Americans. I stop in awkward spots as much, if not more than the young couple across the street wanting to show off their make-out skills. And sometimes, just sometimes, the fact that millions of us are trying to go in completely opposite directions backfires in a way that can only be described as inner-London traffic.

Getting around in London should really have been the new Olympic sport for 2012. It could be called "urban slalom," and you lose points for every biker you hit, every time you disrupt the flow, and maybe even gain a few points for every time you dodge out in front of an oncoming car, knowing full well that you have plenty of time and ample speed to be across by the time the car reaches the crosswalk. The British, of course, would have the home court advantage and make sure that even a New Yorker would get a run for his money. I might just be the champion as I dodge and ram, predicting an entire sidewalk's move and how to avoid a lawsuit while going at top speeds with a 200 kilo electric wheelchair. It's as much art and skill as it is athletics and critical thinking, and I challenge anyone who thinks they can master the London sidewalks to do it on wheels.

Today I found myself in Cambridge Circus, one of my most dreaded areas where Charing Cross meets Tottenham Court Road in an utter mess of confusion and terrible planning. Getting through the crosswalk at Cambridge Circus proves to be the most annoying endeavour in the entire city as buses tend to enjoy stopping for the light directly over the crosswalk, thereby blocking the wheelchair ramp and making it impossible for me to cross the street. Sunglasses on, my iPod in my ears to ensure that nothing would annoy me and I could have a completely private walk in a city of millions, I waited for the stoplight to turn and the crosswalk not to be blocked. Finally an African woman took my hand just as the light was about to change back to "don't walk."

"Come on, honey. We're going."

And with that, she held her hand in front of the oncoming taxi to make sure they would continue to stay still even after the light had changed so I could get across with a clear shot.

Then again, there are some times where you need a city full of strangers just to get by.

WELL PLANNED

BY THE TIME I HAD OPENED my fourth wedding invitation in one week, I was convinced my life was over. I was going to die single, alone, with flowered wallpaper in my flat. I would be at some point in my mid sixties and having had a successful career as an actuary. Because I was an actuary, I would be able to calculate the chances of dying on that particular day and, realising that my odds were increased, I would have laid myself out in the wedding dress I bought at thirty and waited for Death. Of course, what I would've forgotten to consider would be my nine cats. Who, after going three days without food, would begin to eat my face.

Why is it we are always told to plan ahead? In our freshman year of high school we were told to start thinking about colleges. At college we were told on the first day to consider our options for graduate schools. And for my masters, I have to come up with a five-year plan for my career, which to me sounds vaguely like Stalinist Russia. And I know whatever I say, be it I plan to be complete my masters within the standard two years or I want to play Bach while standing on a unicycle at age thirty six, it isn't going to happen. You want to see God laugh? Show her your plans.

The irony of planning ahead is, of course, when things don't go according to plan we feel like failures. The more we know about the path we feel that we have to take, the less confident we are in the direction we are going when we get blown even slightly off course. As a disabled person I can't live alone, but I have no idea with whom I'm living in six months. This is scary. This makes me feel as though I've failed at being an adult because if I don't know how I'm going to eat in six months, then what the heck am I doing in a career as unstable as the arts.

"This is why you need a manslave," my friend begins. She's been engaged for just under a year. I feel like she has her next five years planned out, ready to tick things off of a yellow notepad as she does when we discuss her wedding reception. But then again, she is calling from Russia.

"I've got my own company. That's kinda like having a husband and a baby all rolled into one. I just worry if this deal doesn't go through and the company folds, I'm going to have to live in a nursing home and play card games all day. Maybe I'd be better off doing that though."

"You wouldn't. You can't even hold the cards."

Days like this, I'm in freak-out mode at full force. BBC Radio Fucked plays in my brain at full volume. Life seems too long, an endless series of events and unforeseen occurrences that I can't begin to plan for. Who will be cooking my dinner a year from now? What if I never find an agent? What will I do when my wheelchair dies now that the company has quit making the kind I need? What if I think I find someone, and he leaves me one night with no help?

I can't see past the next hour at this point. And I am well on the road to driving myself to the funny farm while breathing into a paper bag. So I do the one thing I know how to do. I go to the pub.

Another friend is there and he asks me how I am. I'm fine, just like everyone else these days. Big cheesy smile for full effect.

"That good huh? Spill it, missy." He's known me for over five years, and is therefore one of my oldest friends in the city. Which means he's earned the right to hear. Everything. Even the bit about the cats eating my face.

"… And then I think that I have nothing to worry about so I shouldn't feel bad. So of course then I feel worse and worry even more that I'm going crazy." By the time I'm done my friend has every right to bolt.

"Well, that's certainly logical," he states, looking at me.

"How? Was there some day I missed in school where they gave out the secret to handling life?"

"No. No one can see that far ahead in any sort of detail. Really, Athena, looking ahead further than next month is always overwhelming to those of us who are among the living. It's just like acting. We stay in the moment because it's all any of us can do. It's got nothing to do with your disability. We can't hardly take in the now fully. There's too many variables to try and figure out five years from now."

Oh. Now they tell me.

On my way back home I make my way down to the docks to wait for the next ferry. It's cold and I have no idea when the next boat's coming. Maybe I missed the last one. My mind reels off again. I think about everything I want to do this year. How I want to direct *Macbeth* and *Our Town* in rep. The two together would provide an interesting death and rebirth of innocence. After that, I want to call in a new movement teacher for a workshop and perhaps start a new study on neurology and the Alexander Technique ...

The boat is just visible on the eastern edge of the Thames. Its bow light echoing on the surface of the water grows stronger with each passing minute, oblivious to the blackness that it pushes through. It's beautiful in a way I've never noticed before. And I think of what the Stage Manager says to Emily at the end of *Our Town* when the young woman asks if anyone every really sees the beauty of the world while still alive. And the Stage Manager says, "No. The saints and poets, maybe they do some."

And then I smile at how while we're all are straining away to live life, to make something of ourselves, we forget that life is never well planned. And it was never meant to be.

OATHS OF FOOLISHNESS

WHEN I TOLD MY MOM that I would never go back to the UK, she immediately said I would. As I'm on a boat going home, curving around the Thames, that promise seems to have never happened. A lifetime has passed and I am doing exactly what I swore I wouldn't do.

The first time I was in London, I constantly felt as though I was drowning. Going deeper and deeper it was clear that I was not in charge. My assistants were, and I would never be able to take the reins away from them. Before we even left home in Chicago, the tensions were clear, and as we crossed passport control, I kept saying to myself over and over, "Tomorrow I'll wake up and everything will be better. Everything will be as it should be." That summer we would spend three months based in England but also going to various places in Europe while I was completing my research for a thesis. My memories of that time can be best summed up in two words: fear and hunger. Outside of that I don't remember going to the Eiffel Tower or the first time I saw Big Ben. I don't particularly remember the Swiss Alps or being in a bathhouse in Budapest. Fear because one of the assistants was constantly threatening that my chair would go into the river if things didn't go his way. And since every major European city has a river, it was a constant danger. And hunger, because both the assistants saw the fact that I needed help getting food as a way to maintain a level of control. Sometimes it wasn't OK to eat anything. When they felt like it, it was, but the food was minimal.

How I ever got a combination between these two assistants, I don't know, but after I had returned from my journey, several people commented that they knew these individuals better than I did and they immediately thought of it as a bad idea. Why hadn't they said anything before? I will never know. But before I left people encouraged me that these two would be good at keeping a schedule and help me with research. We did indeed follow our complex schedule keeping interviews and seeing resources at an alarming rate. By the end of the summer we had been in no less than 12 countries, and it had all gone exactly as I planned back at the university when I was setting up logistics. It was just that none of it felt the way I had planned it to feel. Several times my assistants told me that I should never leave the United States again because it was so difficult for me to travel and they had to do so much of the work. Six months later I finally had a doctor tell me that what I was facing during that summer was abuse.

When the psychiatrist gave me a diagnosis, I immediately asked if he was sure. "I thought that's what they gave war veterans after being in horrific situations. I've been in nothing of the kind. Just a trip to Europe that didn't go the way I thought it ought to." It would take me years to realise that he was right, that my once insulated world had been shattered. It was almost as if I had a clear demarcation between childhood and adult life. And sometimes, despite the amount of grace for forgiveness I have sought, and successfully obtained, I still wish I could go back to before that world disintegrated.

So, at home, I swore to my family I would never return to the UK. Without thinking, my mother made her response.

The promises we make ourselves when we are in pain are some of the most dangerous oaths we can ever commit to. These promises inevitably shut down our world and shrink life. On one level it makes sense. We are hurting. And who does not cower in the closet when they know there is a monster outside that is too big for them? Mom knew that my oath was quite literally taking the world and shrinking it down to places I would go and places I would not go. When I called her up exactly nine months later telling her that I had gotten an internship that I could not pass up, and I was excited to be moving back to the UK, she wasn't surprised in the least. She always knew that sooner or later I would find the strength somehow to re-open what I had locked away and refused to explore.

We make such promises to ourselves out of fear and self-preservation, two elements in life which should never rule the day. Both of these have their use as we need a bit of safety and stability to ensure our growth. But fear ultimately acts like a thief, forcing us into paralysis and ensuring that our lives are taken away. These oaths of foolishness seem to protect us in the same way headlights protect a deer. They keep us stapled to the ground and stunned, when what we really need to do is move on, if only to avoid the danger of that night. In the end, if we never move, claiming with our entire being that constant lockdown and sworn protection is the only safe way to operate, we never actually get out of danger.

The boat winds around Canary Wharf and is headed towards home. The geometric skyline looks completely mythical and fierce in its proportions compared to the rest of London. I am lucky that, despite my diagnosis, I don't get many flashbacks, and when I do, I can usually control them. I can see my dock as the boat approaches. It's a Tuesday night, which means there is Quiz Night at the pub with people I know and trust. Tomorrow I have an audition followed by a concert with a friend at Saint Martin's It seems impossible that a city in which I felt so much terror could grow within a few years to be my home and is now a place for joy.

I hate to think what would happen if I kept the promises I made to myself while I was in pain.

THE HOPE OF
ROLLER SKATING

I took my first independent steps shortly after I was ten years old. My parents moved into our first house. Unlike our apartment, the house was mostly uncarpeted, which, for someone who is used to crawling as a major mode of transportation, this small detail constituted a major lifestyle change. The difference between crawling on high pile carpet and tile for young knees meant that I learned to walk independently very fast to avoid the inevitable pain of pressing your knees into a completely unforgiving surface. And although I was well on my way to learning how to walk by this point, my mother has later admitted to me that she knew that a tile floor would provide me with the additional incentive needed to learn rapidly.

Of course, I've never been one to do things by halves, so looking back I'm always a little surprised that people had such a reaction when nine months later I had saved enough from my allowance buy a new pair of pink roller skates. The following week I took them to the therapy centre and announced to my physical therapist Sue that I thought learning to roller skate should be my next therapy goal.

My version of "walking" at this point can best be described by that scene when Bambi is attempting to get his feet under him. I wasn't really walking. I had learned to maintain a consistent direction during a controlled fall.

But Sue, the woman who taught me to walk, bought it.

She reached for the roller skates that very afternoon and put them on my feet. Bambi was now trying to maintain a tentative balance while on wheels on ice with a film of motor oil underneath her to make life really interesting. In addition to being on wheels, I was two inches taller than I had ever been. And, having only walked independently for less than a year, I never realised how important having your feet directly underneath you was to walking.

As soon as we went from the treatment room to the clinic hallway, the questions from other therapists began. "What on earth are you doing? Sue, she'll never be able to lean to roller skate. That's not a reasonable therapy goal."

What is the difference between allowing someone to hope and setting them up for disappointment? I've been challenged with this question often by people who are trying to make me "see reality." These people then hide behind the statement, "I just don't want to see you hurt." What they don't see, however, is that I've been hurt already. A lot. And as anyone who has suffered though agonies can tell you, reality fiercely slaps you in the face before you can see it.

Hope is, by definition, something born out of adversity, slim chances, and unquenched desires. We do not hope that our loved ones will come home on time tonight when they've been on time every night for the past year. Unless there is a specific reason as to why tonight is different, we merely expect them to be on time. This is not hope. Hope does not come without the considerable risk of disappointment. Despite what any politician, inspirational speaker, of salesman may want you to believe, you cannot offer people hope without running the risk of their facing disappointment; the two will always go hand in hand.

Now there will be many who will respond to this by claiming that there is a world difference between giving hope to someone to obtain a reasonable goal and encouraging someone to reach for an unreasonable goal. In the forthcoming weeks Sue was challenged with this statement plenty. In addition to roller skating being an unreasonable goal, it was deemed something even worse: not useful. After all, what possible use could I have for roller-skating? Wouldn't my time be better spent learning to climb stairs or completing some goal which would otherwise prove to be a hindrance in the real world?

This argument suddenly kept popping up much more in my life when I decided to become an actor. Was my being onstage really a reasonable goal? After all, "you're just so intelligent, performing seems like it would be such a waste. Have you thought about being a lawyer instead?"

But the argument of anything being a reasonable or even useful goal depends on the honest answer of a single question: according to whom? Like anything else, is the judgment of a single person (or even a group) enough to make that declaration true? Someone may judge a dream unreasonable because they are unwilling to make the sacrifices it would take for it to come true. Others may deem it as a waste of resources simply because qualities such as intelligence, strength, and specific abilities are not his to offer or make use of. But that doesn't mean that a goal was ever unreachable. It simply means that that person was unwilling to do what it took to attain it. But one man's limitations should never be placed on another, self-imposed or otherwise.

At the age of four, just before I started working with Sue, my mother sat in a meeting with my school's administrators in which she was informed that I would never be encouraged to walk during school. Their justification was that encouraging me to walk was an unreasonable goal. Despite my mother's protests and evidence none of the administrative experts or physical therapists would concede. Finally a student teacher raised her hand and said that she would give up her lunch hour to teach me skills I would need for walking. She never got to see me walk without the walker that she had to tape my hands to. She never saw me on roller-skates. But something told her those efforts were not wasted.

One wonders what the school's reaction would be if my mother had brought in a pair of skates.

No man is ever made to live his life as he would wear a hand-me-down pair of shoes. It is not the role of anybody else to break in the seams and canvas of the pair of cross trainers, and then hand them back to you explaining what they are and are not capable of. That is your task, nobody else's.

What Sue realised and other therapists did not, is that even though I would never be a roller derby queen, there were things to be learned which roller-skating exemplified. Things like flexing one's hips, finding core strength, regaining a centre of gravity, and even the coordination it takes to bring one foot consistently in front of the other all are skills which a pair of skates can challenge you to master more than being on your own two feet. Like football players taking ballet lessons to improve their game, Sue never expected me to become a great skater. And if I had become one that point would be moot. What she was interested in was that I learned how to walk to the best of my ability. And if it took a pair of roller skates to learn that, then who was to say that roller skating did not lend itself to a reasonable therapy goal?

Eventually I lost interest in the roller skates. I think I brought in a bike instead. And when I got my permit, Sue and a few other therapists took me out to learn to drive. Which is pretty impressive given that I came to the therapy centre with the expectation of accomplishing the skills of grunting and being able to sit up independently back when I was six months old. It is the people who refuse to stop because hope may bring disappointment, refuse to believe that any dream is unreasonable, and strive for something which is deemed useless, who have the richest lives and greatest victories. The people who live life safely, refusing to reach beyond what is within easy grasp, have no claim on the lives of those who do.

After I was halfway through college, I went back to the therapy center for a visit. Walking down the hall, I saw a small boy grasping desperately at the wall for balance. He was trying to move forward despite being attached to a set of roller skates. At a closer look, I saw they were the adjustable kind which attached to shoes. They bore the initials of the therapy clinic. Long after Sue had left, some therapist obviously thought they would be a good investment for teaching disabled children. The boy's own therapist was encouraging him to move away from the wall. In answer to his protests and fears of falling she said, "Yeah, so what? Not like you haven't fallen before." I couldn't help but smile.

Those who refuse to fall cannot learn to walk. They will look at a pair of brand new roller skates and never try them on. And eventually, they will do everything possible not to let a loved one fly. Doesn't matter, they gave up the option to advise you as soon as they refused even to take a single risk of their own.

BEAUTY UNSUSPECTED

‡⇌ ⇌‡

I WEAR THE TOP BUTTON OF MY JEANS unbuttoned at all times. For most women this would make me a slut, but in my case it just makes me pathetic. Today, I have funky red hair, I'm 5' 2", one hundred pounds, a 30-F, Banana Republic size zero. I have blue eyes, eyelashes so long I can't wear sunglasses, lovely skin, and a smile that never stops. I've been schooled in classics, theology, philosophy, Spanish, Arabic, ballet, athletics, kinesiology, theatre, karate, and politics. I've travelled to twenty counties, broken five international track and field records, and taught school in Mexico.

Like what you're reading? I'll go on. I've got a cute butt, an absurdly long tongue for cocktail party tricks, a set of wheels custom made for me, and a great sense of humour. I'm an hourglass figure, à la Marilyn Monroe, very flexible, and ready to embrace the true meaning of freedom.

All of this and I've never been asked out on a date.

Which doesn't mean I don't get any action. Every time I go to the airport I get pulled out of line and patted down by some security guard, their gloved hands running up and down my most intimate areas. The last time I was in Boston one hefty, uniformed individual whispered into my ear, "This is my favourite part about my job. I'm so good at it," as she rubbed her hand up the inside of my leg.

Come fly the 'friendly' skies.

After years of living with a disability, I am still constantly amazed by how sexually frustrated young disabled women are. I've seen girls with all types of disabilities burst into tears and held them time and again as they sobbed, "But I'll never have a boyfriend." Often it seems as if perceived asexuality is the greatest disappointment from disability as I watch young women yearn to feel beautiful, desire a man's touch, wish to have the freedom and confidence to invite him back to their room for the night. Just like all women, we too crave to feel cherished.

It is particularly difficult to watch idealised images of love, even though my brain knows that these ideals will falter, fall flat on their faces, and cause more heartache that I can ever imagine. I remember coming home after a bridal shower for two friends last year and sobbing in the bath, "I want to be loved like that. I want to be held like he holds her. I want to be someone's sexual dream. I want so badly to be given dishtowels by my best friend and be excited about them."

Lots of people tell me I should "just go for it," as if love was something you could just reach out and snatch. And it would, certainly, send a loud message. But it isn't my style. I'm not willing to put anyone in the hard position of turning down a disabled woman. And, call me old fashioned, but any man who sees me as asexual or who isn't willing to go after what he wants, doesn't deserve me. After all, if he can't do that, life with all its dramas and growing pains is going to be impossible to navigate as a couple. And so I wait, sometimes bearing the expectation well, and other days not.

Impatiently waiting does have a wonderful advantage though. I may cry every time I see Cyrano de Bergerac, but I am able to take the time many girls use to primp and throw themselves ruthlessly at guys to excel at everything I wish to do. And I know I have been given desire that only certain men are man enough to fill. True, pure hunger is made to be satisfied.

Unlike many of my disabled peers, I know my inactive romantic life is actually not my fault. Indeed, it's amazing how guys who do not know about the disability will give me complements without hesitation. On the way back from the tube today I looked out the car window to see a car full of guys whopping and yelling at me, making eye contact and wagging their tongues in my direction. In Switzerland this summer, during a particularly hard evening, I opened my third story window and stood alone watching the sunset on the balcony. Within a few moments a Swiss walked by, stopping to stare at me. He yelled up, first in French, then Italian, then German. After all attempts failed he tried English. "You are the most beautiful vision I have even seen. I wish I had a camera to make your picture. May I come up to see you?" Unaccustomed to such attention, I always smile and back away, knowing that mystery is more romantic than exposure.

I am beautiful. I am sexy. I will be cherished by a man someday. I don't need to waste my time with false lovers, for I know I have these characteristics, even if no one else suspects it.

WHEN THE DOORS OPENED

⇥ ⇤

OK SO ... IT'S 8:30 IN THE MORNING and I'm rushing through the train station trying to reach the 8:38 to Norwich. It's pouring rain outside and everything that could go wrong has gone wrong. Naturally I think, *"Good, glad I got all the bad luck out of the way."*

Or that's what I was stupid enough to believe.

As I swivel into the elevator a priest comes in behind me. I know who he is because he's in full garb. I quickly start off: *Dear Lord please don't make him start praying to heal me. I never know what to say when they start praying ...* He gets off at the next floor without even 'God bless.' Apparently he's not on duty yet. I go down one more floor to get off myself. At least in theory that's what's supposed to happen.

Once down to my floor I am met by a large lump. I stop dead. It's completely blocking my path to get out of the lift. I can't move it myself. *What a stupid and unthoughtful place to leave stuff. If I ruled the world there would be none of this ...* My electric wheelchair bars the door from closing as I look around the ticket hall for someone to move the obstacle.

"Um ... Excuse me, sir ..." I flag down a security guard and do my best damsel-in-distress act. I can still make the 8:38 with very little luck needed. Or there is the 9:08. I laboriously do the math in my head. I haven't had enough sugar to do higher mathematics as of yet. I need my morning hot chocolate. The guard comes and starts to move the pile of rubbish out of the elevator frame. Then, at the exact same time he and I come to the exact same realisation.

It's a corpse.

He drops what we now realise to be an arm and I jump back into the lift without foreseeing that this action will make the impatient door shut. The guard is now leaning over the body trying to stop the door from closing because, of course, he doesn't want anyone else to come down in the lift and get an early morning surprise. Without thinking, I pull the emergency stop button which makes everything better ... for about two seconds. Then the elevator alarm sounds thus bringing this situation to more people's attention.

There is nothing I can do to think what the next course of action should be. There is no precedent. I don't think that there has ever been a Miss Manners column to date about what the classy thing to do is once you have become impeded by a corpse. I begin to think two things. First I feel sorry for the poor man who has died in Liverpool Street Station during the wee morning hours. And second, if my mother ever makes me take the etiquette lesson she's threatening me with, I am so asking about this in class.

By the time we've cleared him out of the way, I'm being bombarded with questions by other station staff. Why is he there? How long has he been there? Do I know him? Will I come down to the office and answer some questions? They want to detain me and investigate into the issue further. So it's bye-bye 9:08 train to Norwich, as I call my professor and try to explain what has happened. Mid explanation, I am told to put down to phone and please pay attention to the very serious matter at hand.

"I don't know anything. The elevator door just opened and there he was!" Some brilliant officer comments that it seems like an unlikely story. Yeah, you're telling me.

"Look, which is more likely: that the elevator doors just opened and there he was or I have clobbered this man who is twice my size and am now dragging the corpse with me as luggage on the way to Norwich hoping people won't notice." I very quickly shut myself up realising that until about a half hour ago, I would have thought that one situation was as absurd as the other, and yet here we were. The police ask me if I'd like anything to drink. Which seems a very odd thing to do for a potential murder suspect but sometimes I still have to throw in the towel when it comes to comprehending English customs. What I really wanted was a Belgian hot chocolate from Cafe Nero with whipped cream and extra marshmallows on top, the one that I was intending to get when I was getting out of the lift, but somehow this didn't seem like the right answer. So I answered with the obligatory tea with milk, no sugar which I never got either because they quickly looked at the CCTV footage and determined I wasn't a murderer.

For several weeks now I've been trying to come up with some higher meaning for the whole incident. I keep thinking this must be a metaphor for something. But I've had no luck with coming up with an answer. Life just is messy and sometimes you don't know what file to put something under. Was it tragic for whoever he was? Was it comedy? Can one negate the other? My path to school that day crossed with someone else's path out of this world. And for a while he was in my way. And then he wasn't. Sometimes in life there is no acceptable response. We just have to face the truth and then catch a later train than we had originally intended.

HER PORTRAIT OF ME

⊱ ⊰

DURING MY TWENTIETH YEAR I developed the remarkable ability to lose time. I sat in my dorm room and watched the wall, hoping that nothing would happen. And then my roommate would come in and ask me down to dinner, forcing me to look at my clock and see that over four hours of my life had gone missing. Sometimes I would find myself in a bathtub full of water staring at my razor blade at 3:30 in the morning, having no idea how I got there. It was as though little green men had come and taken me, the essence of who I was, and left a shell which was too stupid to know to stop. And because I kept going through the motions, everyone thought I was fine.

By the time four months slipped away from me (according to the calendar) I was gone. Everything that was characteristic about me had vanished. I couldn't even recognise my own body in a mirror. I had a diagnosis, which frankly may as well have been in Japanese. I knew what it was called; I had read about it during AP Psychology in high school. I knew the literary context of it from English classes. I knew back then this particular diagnosis only developed in extreme circumstances. Back when I was eighteen I was arrogant enough to know that I would never get such a condition. Now I knew that logic was wrong. I knew all these facts; I just didn't know what to do about it.

I "snapped out of it" to find myself lying down on the back pew at our campus church. I heard singing. I heard bongos. I pieced together that I was at our Thursday night worship service. It was Thursday. Huh, who knew? I stayed there staring up at the ceiling, too heavy to move. People walked out by me. Suddenly my friend Ashley came into my vision.

Her Portrait of Me

"I need you to pose nude for me this weekend."

"What?"

"I need you to pose nude for me this weekend. I've asked nearly every one of my friends and nobody has the balls to do it. I have a painting due next week. So now I'm telling you. I need you to pose nude for me this weekend." I don't know what I was expecting Ashley to say, maybe "You look tired" or "I'm worried about you." This wasn't how most people climbed out of the depths of despair. But I agreed.

For most women, the idea of stripping off all of their clothes and letting someone sit there with an easel and study them is horrifying. Not for me. Body image is, unbelievably, one of the few struggles I have never had to deal with. Maybe it comes from the fact that my body is utterly uncooperative anyway. As a movement teacher in drama school once told me: "You can just tell. Your brain says, 'Do it,' and your body says, 'Fuck you.'"

All of which was probably just as well at this point. I have no recollection of that Friday and when I "snapped out of it" again, I was lying on my side, Ashley readjusting my hair over my bare shoulder, my arm straining to reach the edge of sunlight. She looked at me with the eyes of an artist, selecting what to paint and highlight as a metaphysical recreation. Her eyes shifted back and forth from the canvas to my skin with the level of observation of a scientist. Her brown hair fell into her eyes every few minutes when she forgot herself.

To let someone paint you, see you without obstacles and barriers and then interpret it for an audience, means they know everything. Not simply every scar or mole, but she knows you from observation and study, much like a scientist would know his subject. And yet she deems you a worthy subject not just to reproduce but reflect upon and learn from. As I stared up at the ceiling, feeling the ruffles of the cloth underneath me, I felt at rest. For the first time in months I didn't have to explain or excuse anything. She just spoke quietly about her own thoughts and reactions so I could gather my own.

Sometimes it takes being naked and having nothing to regain something. That day I got the smallest part of myself and my pride

Her Portrait of Me

back. This is me. I need nothing else. It's okay to be naked and have no excuses. Within this feeble state you will be made perfect.

And I sat there, naked, aware of every moment. I still haven't forgotten a second of those three hours in November.

MORDICHAI

I USED TO SPEND MY MORNINGS with a man I called Mordichai. True to his namesake, he is considered an outcast even by certain members of my own family. I would sneak into his room before classes began in high school and try to warm my hands, wounded from a combination of the harsh Chicago cold and the reality of living in a wheelchair. Looking to him for a combination of wisdom and simple sanity, I would sit at Mordichai's desk to write, to read, or simply to try to sort through the inner workings of an eighteen-year-old's brain. Each year I grew a bit older, but it seemed as if he did not. Rather, with each passing year we became closer in age; I learned more of his reality and he learned more of my secrets.

Growing up alongside Mordichai and his partner Tom provided me with grace and an added level of support to the already strong scaffolding that my parents gave me. They were a couple with whom I would disagree fiercely and still know that I was loved ... perhaps loved even more because I had the strength to disagree. As time went on, our conversations revolved more around big topics, which were out of my grasp when I first met them as a fifteen year old. Questions of freedom and liberty, morality and common good haunted us some nights as our meeting venue changed from his classroom to the fireplace in his own home. I was now living independently, working part time, and continuing with my education at the university level.

And as questions became easier to grasp, the answers grew increasingly slippery, until one day it occurred to us both that our world is not limitless, and the entitled freedoms that we were promised, presumably by either God or by the most basic human rights, have yet

26

to be delivered in full. My world had to stop at the first unpaved road I came upon if my wheelchair could not cross it. For Mordichai and Tom, what was everyone else's private business was still held in court, amongst a blaze of furious protesters and a network news frenzy, waiting for a decision that seemed obvious to me.

In many ways I am jealous of the media's attention to Mordichai's issues over my own. And who can blame the broadcasters? The image of an angered drag queen will no doubt get more viewers than that of a group of paraplegics crawling up the steps of the US Capitol building at an abrasively slow rate. What's worse is that as a disabled person, my rights are constantly pitted up against other causes, such as the new environmentally-friendly taxi cabs which, in order to save on fuel, have been made so small that no wheelchair will ever be able to fit inside. It's an either / or society. The same week that Mordichai's right to have his partner visit him in the hospital gets debated on national television back in the US, the American with Disabilities Act gets stripped by the Supreme Court and nobody notices.

"This is why you're a writer. That's why you always need to have your pen, and hands that are at the ready." Mordichai's voice echoes in my ear. To give a voice to a community that is still relatively unheard sometimes feels like trying to remove barnacles with one's bare hands. To find my own voice on top of that challenge can prove to be as effective as a screen door on a submarine some days. Sometimes I think we all wish we could finish growing up before the troubles come.

I went back to visit Mordichai a few weeks ago. The winter wind is nowhere near leaving Chicago in April, and I can feel a film of salt covering my hands as I come inside. He asks me how I am, and I don't know where to begin. When did life scatter in a thousand different directions? I start with the most obvious, "My hands hurt from this horrible weather. How do you stand it?"

"I'm not in a wheelchair," he begins. We all have that one thorn in our side, which we wish to have removed. And yet it painfully stays there to shape our world.

Without speaking he gets up and leaves, only to return with a bottle of lotion that smells of sandalwood. He puts some on my hands and rubs it in. He starts muttering about how I should be taking better care of myself, about how I only have so many units of energy per day to spend and I should be more selective in the battles I fight. Sometimes having him around is like having a second father. I argue with him and protest about the lotion, if for no other reason then it's my role to do so. It doesn't matter because we're both convinced we are right. I need my hands not to be greasy so I can go places and be just like everyone else. He stops me there.

My hands, he reminds me, should be used for writing about issues and images in a voice no one has heard before.

BAREFOOT BENEATH MY FEET

ON THE RARE DAYS that I have the balance to walk, I choose to do so barefoot, even if it means that I compromise my stability in the process. Grant you, those days are exceedingly rare and when they do come, I am like a child again, constantly making discoveries that my peers have forgotten long ago. I was eighteen when I first felt the morning dew from the grass on the bottom of my feet. I was walking across a freshly mowed field in the foothills of North Carolina, a friend on each side, when the crystal drops kissed my feet. Each little drop held an entire universe of colour and science as it baptised my feet with the fresh water of the new morning haze.

Two years later I found myself walking along the southern beaches of the Carolinas, again firmly supported by two more friends. Never before had my feet sunk into the sand, been covered by a compound so vast, or felt the entire earth move beneath my feet. I had no sense of the ground I was walking on, what crevasse the sand and splinters would next inhabit my foot, and everything beneath my step was alive. The shells, the critters, everything that the ocean pulled in was full of vibrant life compared to everything I felt on my sole. Walking barefoot connected me to the rest of all that was in existence rather than that same metal plate that held my feet day in and day out. When I did not walk, what I felt beneath my feet was only the same five inches of steel day after day.

And so, when I stood to feel the life beneath my feet, the new discoveries were made with two other souls by my side holding me up from the ground. Such souls who had felt the life move beneath their feet when they were still stumbling to walk neglected their discoveries now. It was a period of their life which had passed long ago and they had since forgotten. But now they were serving me by walking me across such an unknown landscape, not just helping me get to my destination, but unknowingly allowing me to explore a new corner of a complex life. To the people walking beside me, it was the place I was trying to get to that was the important service. Any new discoveries I made along the way were side effects.

Often I think when people look at me, they see an opportunity to serve, to have a good deed done for the day. While I do need more help than most, my independence is all the more valuable to me when it comes to the very limited amount of things that I can do. Many of my friends call it stubborn when I try for minutes to open a can of soda or put on a jacket, but it's so much more for me than that. Every mundane accomplishment is a declaration that I am here, that my actions are strong and that I am still a force moving and shaping this chaotic world. Reduce me to someone merely to be served and I am worthless except when it comes time for you to feel good about yourself.

And yet, as an individual of faith, I am bound to appreciate the people who offer me help. To serve another is to knit me together with my fellow man in an offering to the transcendent truth that is merciful to us all, or so they say from the pulpit. But I, in my frail humanity, am often considered one to be served rather than offer service to another. I sit in the simple wooden pew and even in the silence feel the questions bore inside my skull from the rest of the congregation. Now I feel connected to all around me only because 10,000 inquisitions bounce around in my head from being trapped inside like a thoughtful superball. Should I? How much pain? How long? What can I do to help? The answer: I'm fine. I got here by myself, didn't I?

However, let me challenge you for just a moment in a way that drives the Western world mad: let me serve you. I am not just someone to be served when I need it and when it is convenient to you. I do not only exist at Christmas or when the charity bucket gets hung up for donations outside some Walmart chain. Therein lies the true shame of it all ... here is the true tragedy of disability, if you will: Are we not all equal? And as equals are we not required to pull our own weight so that not only do you feed me dinner because I need to eat, but then, I can hold your head when you're fighting from going under. My hands still work, my heart is not yet at peace, and I yearn to effect this world as much as you do. I want to shape the ground that my feet walk upon.

A few weeks ago, we held a foot washing ceremony during the worship service I go to every Thursday night. The service is simple in that Calvinist sort of way that only can come from years of struggling with calloused hands and aching muscles. The feeling and optimism come from hard work and from biting into the impossible while trying to swallow the world whole. The sanctuary is dimly lit by flickering candles reflected against the whitewashed walls and simple oak pews. Our water basins are not made of glass or silver, just sturdy plastic so that the containers can have a myriad of unexpected uses. The towels we use are old and have seen everything from rainy days and the bottom of muddy boots to hot pans from an oven. The tools are meagre, but like so many things in life, the more meagre something is, the better it feeds your insides.

The Christian tradition of foot washing is one of my favourite actions. It's not a ritual, requirement, or even retribution. It's just a form of service taken from the ancient days when everything that was in the world (rocky, soft, or just plain disgusting) touched the bottoms of a man's feet. For me, that's the tenderest area of the body, mainly from years of inexperience. However, when a host did not wash the feet of his guests, that was a sign not only of dirty floors but of a hard heart as well.

I dipped my feet in the warm water and prepared to lift them up by request. I looked at yet another friend who had gotten me up countless mornings, fed me a multitude of meals and caught me from falling both physically and emotionally. Without thinking, I got out of the tub and knelt beside her, every bone of my foot pressing into the wooden floor. I did not worry about splinters or even sores in my feet. I only wanted her to know that she was loved. The warm waters of the bucket felt more soothing on my hands than it did on my feet. Though I felt that every eye in the room was watching me, I did not mind that I was feeling such discomfort. I knew I had not completed the act of washing her feet because I wanted everyone to see what a stellar servant I was; I did not mean to get on the floor for my own comfort, because if it were up to me I would be doing it in a closet. I washed her feet to understand her life, her way of travelling the world, and the places her feet had taken her that mine had not.

WHAT I KNOW OF HER SON

SHE IS A WOMAN WHOM I have been wanting to meet for years. Ever since I first heard my friend describe his mother, I knew two things about her. First, I knew that she was amazing just by examining my friend's outlook on life. And second, that she had a degenerative nerve disease. When he speaks of his mother, my friend keeps the latter fact quiet and simple, telling me of what she's done and what she used to tell him.

"She's fine ... Well she's not fine—she has a nerve disease. But it really doesn't affect her that much." And so, when I finally bumped into her visiting her son while walking down the road at a Sunday pace, I was surprised as she was further along in her condition than he had made it out to sound. As close as we were, I wish he had told me honestly of her troubles. But maybe he is as blind to her disability as he is to mine.

I'm always intrigued when I meet someone's parents as it usually explains a lot. Most of the time I meet the family members of my loved ones and I think, "Ah, that makes a good deal of sense." Although there is the occasional meeting which yields the question, "Where on earth did you come from?" For the most part, I walk away from meeting Mom and Dad understanding my friends a little bit more, and thus holding our friendship in even greater esteem. I am particularly excited when it comes to spending time with someone's mother. Mothers open up the world to their children, making the entire universe more inclusive. I have met all of this woman's children and I can safely say that she did a wonderful job in raising them.

My friend is her second eldest son, and was raised particularly well. For my own sake, when I am out with him it is as close as I can possibly imagine to being fully independent. I don't feel disabled in his company, nor do I feel as if I have to work with some foreign party, striking bargains between my desires and his willingness. As close as a friend can be, he lets me utterly forget my limitations and explore a world with more scope than I knew possible. Such abilities almost always come from the influence of the parents.

As soon as we were introduced, her eyes lit up with a flicker of recognition. She was holding onto her walker and instantly called me by name. From this I gathered that she somehow knew me and that I was a familiar character in their home. Seeing her watch my friend, her son, handle my bags and meet my needs, it suddenly dawned on me that this behaviour she was witnessing in the young man that she helped raise, nurse, feed and carry was new to her. She probably never saw anyone reliant on him as I am on a regular basis. The fact is, I depend on all of my friends, but particularly him, and I forget that this often looks strange to the outside world.

Then, almost instantly, I came to another realisation, that because of her own disability someday soon she will be dependent on him as well. For many individuals with a long-term degenerative illness, this impending dependency is the most terrifying thing to overcome. At that point in time, how you, as a parent, raised your children will influence how they will take care of you. It is a classic example of an individual reaping what he sows. As parents teach their children to care for human life and value it, they must see that eventually they will be under the care of their children in one form or another. Those families who do not bother to teach their children such values and ethics will no doubt feel it when the older generation inevitably starts losing its own independence.

I am at an age where just about everyone I know is having to face human weakness in a very real way. Ten years ago, when I was still a teenager and the world had yet to face many of the struggles which we are still sorting through today, most of my friends had two perfectly healthy parents, and the sickest any of them had ever been was a eight week long bout of the kissing disease. I was the one with the odd perspective, knowing that our bodies do not obey our every command forever, and that it is our fragility and codependence which makes us capable of such astounding beauty. My friends today are just on the edge of realising that there is no such thing as self-sufficiency, that their bodies will decay, and, what is scarier still, their parents' bodies are well on the way to becoming the stuff of earth. My friends often look to me in order to determine how to operate in a world full of their own feebleness and how to care for the loved ones who are suddenly in need. I know they learn how to take care of people well by being my friend, and I am honoured they get to learn these skills as a result of my own needs. It is in tending to the weaknesses and hurts of our loved ones, that we can strengthen ourselves for the inevitable struggles which are to come.

In looking at the mother of one of my best friends, I was humbled to know something about her children, particularly her son, that she knew nothing of. She has never been directly under the care of her children. I rely on her son almost daily. In this small way, I know, first hand, how her son looks out for people in need. I know he is unafraid to feed someone when a spoon becomes too difficult to hold onto. I have had her children tie my shoes without breaking the conversation. I know that the ethics and values she taught her son aren't just hypothetical. They translate into concrete action.

Some days I wish I could tell her now that when her body rebels and she is no longer able to do what was once considered a natural reflex without a massive amount of frustration, she will have no need to worry. I wish I could tell her all the ways that I see my friend stepping up to the plate and preparing himself to take care of his parents when they grow older. I wish I could tell her the stories of all the times he has advocated for me, and that I am grateful to have such a fabulous friend.

But if she and her husband raised their children to become such incredible people, perhaps she has know what he is capable of all along.

THE LANGUAGE OF WORSHIP
AND ACHE

It was late at night when I finally began to think about suffering. The lights were going out and I was sitting in my favourite spot in the flat looking at the Thames go by on the staircase. I thought, "Nobody likes to suffer." Earlier that week there had been flashing lights and sirens on the bridge that crosses an area of our local quay. The road was blocked off for hours, and we had to go the long way around the neighbourhood in order to visit our local supermarket and shopping centre. After it was finally cleared away, four bouquets of flowers had been tied to posts of the barricade which prevents people from falling into the river. An eleven-year-old boy had jumped in on a hot summer's day and on the way down, hit his head against the wall causing him to lose consciousness. It took two hours for emergency crew to find his body.

My pirate friends, when they reported this to me at the pub, kept saying over and over, "We told those kids not to play there; not to jump in." I could see the frustration that comes with age and understanding dangers that children remain ignorant of to or choose to ignore. I don't think they would be as upset if a seventeen-year-old had done the same thing, but a child ... My friends were visibly frustrated.

If you live long enough, you will be miserable. It doesn't matter how much money you have or how protected your life is. It's a fact of the human condition; you will suffer. And you will be tested in how much you are determined that life is worth living. The alternative is that you die young, as the case of our neighbour boy. In that case you inevitably make a bunch of other people miserable. Such is the depressing side of the circle of life. We love; we grow attached to people, things, ideas, places, and they are inevitably taken away and we are given the choice to clutch on thereby suffocating ourselves and the people around or let go thereby accepting the pain, accepting change and forcing ourselves never to have any stability at all.

A book I was reading not too long ago explained that a sociologist interviewed the victims who had survived the Jewish concentration camps of the second World War to ask what effect the experience had on their faith. The findings were shocking:

> "During the 1970's, a man named Reeve Robert Brenner surveyed 1000 survivors of the Holocaust, enquiring especially about their religious faith. How had the experience of the Holocaust effected their beliefs about God? Somewhat astonishingly almost half claimed that the Holocaust had no effect on their beliefs about God. But the other half told a different story. Of the total number surveyed, 11 percent said they had rejected all belief in the existence of God as a direct result of their experience. After the war they never regained faith. Analyzing their detailed responses, Brenner noted that their professed atheism seemed less a matter of theological belief and more of an emotional reaction, an expression of deep hurt and anger against God for abandoning them" (From: *Where Is God When It Hurts* by Phillip Yancey).

Suffering in any form forces us to reevaluate our ideas about the bedrock of what we base our life on. For the eleven percent of people who became atheists as a result of their experience, it means taking a good long hard look at one's own religion, turning around, and walking away. For others it means undergoing that same examination of one's beliefs and deciding if they are worth keeping, need to be re-edited, or need to be thrown out entirely. Assuming that there is a God out there, many of us think that it must be pretty easy being in control of the entire universe. One can look at the Old Testament as well as the Torah and characters such as Moses and Abraham who believed in an absolute God with an enormous personality. These were individuals who said to their creator, "Sure it's easy being up there. Why don't you come down here for a bit and try it out, huh?"

As humans, when we think about God, we are torn between two dichotomies. The first is we want Him to suffer. We want Him to know how difficult life is if He is out there, and do everything He can to improve it. But the irony of it is, if there is a God, do we have any room in our human ideology for a God that willingly sacrifices and goes through agony? We can't stand the idea of a God who lives above us oblivious to the concept of human pain and suffering, and yet the idea that an all powerful being that would willingly submit Himself to such agony and pain completely out of love is outside our concept of what God is. We have no classification for a God who feels pain by choice. Perhaps it's a contradiction of terms, someone who is almighty and chooses the difficult way.

I think about the family of the little boy who jumped into the water two weeks ago, how much suffering they must be going through now. The truth is not only do I hate it; I get every bit as angry as my friends.

A child didn't live long enough to suffer, and ironically that's what angers us all. The fact is that his life was cut short on a whim. Now his family is left picking up the pieces, asking the questions which inevitably come from suffering and searching for answers.

In this way the child is very much like our preconception of God. We want every child to live long enough to know what suffering is and to ask questions about life himself rather than asking them in the wake of a child's death. But ironically, like everyone else, we know that it would be much simpler if neither God, nor the child, nor anyone else had to suffer in the first place.

THROUGH FIRE AND
FRIENDSHIP

＋≒ ≒＋

By THE TIME THE PHONE WAS RINGING on the other end of the line I
questioned whether or not he ever wanted to hear from me again. It
had been two years to the day since we last spoke and that conversation
had not ended well. "Come back," he had said to me. "Move to New
York and ..." For him the answers seemed so easy. To me they sounded
trite. I screamed, he pushed back, and then nothing. That conversation
was over and we went our separate ways.

The sound of an American telephone ringing its single long ring
sounded foreign to me now. I had dialed the long-remembered number
with a shaky hand after reading the news. His entire house had burned
to the ground seven days before from being struck by lightning. And
while no one was home on that fateful night, including his two dogs,
nothing could be saved from the rubble. I called him out of gut reaction,
thinking of his home and the beautiful things in it. In my younger days
he had always seemed to me to be The Great Gatsby himself, with the
exact home and life I had wanted. Yet, when he had invited me to leave
London and move to New York under his care two years ago I had
rejected him furiously, in a justified rage that burned out of control
and smouldered for far too long. I hadn't wanted his life for quite some
time. I had my own. I am happy now, in London. Each day I find that
my roots grow deeper here, stabilising me in a place I am certain, for
now at least, is my home. I had burned bridges with him to stay here.
Now I wondered if he would let me swim back to meet him.

I wasn't expecting him to pick up. He's the type of man you always
have to try a hundred and sixty seven times to get ahold of until it

happens. I gasped his name and he shouted mine. And then the line went dead. Did he really hate me that much or had Skype failed me yet again? A screen popped up on my computer asking me a simple question: "Please tell us how you would rate your call?"

AWFUL. MISERABLE. I want to hunt down the moron who invented Skype this very moment and rip out his toenails after chucking my iMac into the River Thames. Somehow this wasn't an option. I clicked cancel and redialled.

He picked up and said my name first this time.

"Tell me what I can do to help you."

"Nothing. Wait. No. Call me at this exact same time tomorrow."

"Okay," I said reaching for my iPhone and wondering what meeting I had to cancel to make this call.

"Oh and, I'm sorry I have been such a crummy friend lately."

"Me too." We hung up. I couldn't remember who forgave whom.

"We are rebuilding," he told me confidently. "It'll take years to get it back to where it was, but we want to do it. I feel obliged in a way. It was such a lovely house and just added so much to the town." I knew he was right. The home had most likely been featured in a plethora of home and garden magazines in the past two years. He had always loved opening his home up to people. I could tell that being able to offer hospitality was what he was missing the most. "And when it's all done we'll have the biggest party you can imagine." I already knew I wanted to be there.

He and I spoke for over an hour, which, for a man fielding calls from insurance people while trying to rebuild his life, is a very long time. I told him of my own fires over the past years, more metaphorical than his, perhaps, but every bit as searing. Two years ago he caught me at the front end of it. These fires were far from being put out, but at least for now they seemed to be under control.

"It sounds to me as if there is more than one way to burn a house," his voice had changed dramatically. He was right. My own fires had

40

forced me to stay here. Even when he could not comprehend it, I had to stay in London. I could not go 'home.' There was no home to go back to anymore.

There was the ash and rubble of the past several years. There were times of playing the fiddle while the flames raged on because there was nothing left to do. From all of this I had stumbled out, changed and transformed into a woman rather than the teenage girl he met thirteen years before. A few short years ago I thought fires shouldn't happen. Now I'm a bit better at calmly walking through them without getting burned. Maybe if he had been around the flames wouldn't have gotten so high and enveloped me as much. But then again, without it all burning down, I wouldn't have to get up out of the ashes and rebuild either. Now that we had reconnected after two years I was his equal. And when everything goes up in smoke around you, sometimes what you need most is a friend who has also gone through the rubble and made it out the other side.

"You are exactly where you belong." The silence was deafening on my end as I let these words sink it. This was what I longed to hear him say these past two years. It was all over. This fire had been smothered, the rubble cleared, and out of the ashes and destruction from two years ago came a new and stronger friendship, made purer by the flames.

"Let me know if I can do anything for you." Things were winding down and I just wanted to reach out and hold him in whatever way I could.

"I think you just did," was all he said.

I hung up, telling Skype that my call was 'excellent with no problems.'

THE SIRENS

I'M GUESSING IT'S RARE FOR MOST PEOPLE to have a complete stranger inform them that their old home was the perfect spot for skinny dipping. Add to that situation that I was at a wedding when I was informed of this fact and you may get some clue of just how bizarre my life actually is. But maybe I should back up a little bit.

My last year of college I lived on Lake Norman, foreshadowing my obsession with living on water in subsequent years. We were surrounded by docks and walkways which made for amazing spring evenings and nighttime strolls spent battling bug bites. It was from the back porch that I wrote my thesis and various plays which were desperate to be born. And it was just the beginning of November when my friend Cristi and I discovered that the dock in my back yard had its lights burned out. Which made it the perfect place for skinny dipping,

Now I figure if peer pressure can be blamed for kids using drugs or drinking alcohol, there must be somewhere in the book that says you can blame it for suddenly finding yourself swimming naked in a lake at midnight just four weeks before Christmas. We left our terry cloth bathrobes in a pile on the planked wood while each of us did our best to slip silently into the cold autumn water without giving any sign of the icy shock. Our still changing figures cast shadows in the night as we discovered curves and lines we never knew we had. A waist which was still hidden under baby fat last summer, breasts we still crossed our arms to hide, all the insecurities of a teenager were still evident and eventually had to be stripped away through a combination of proximity to other people and water which was so cold, it was violent.

Many girls hit puberty at ten or twelve, and we look like women long before we feel like it. By college the rest of the world expected me to act like a woman, and I had no idea what that meant. Refusing to look down when we got into the shower, we hid under t-shirts and basketball shorts or, on some evenings, under the dock in a huddle, as a man with a dog walked by. Most people assume that for young women, body image issues stem from a lack of self-esteem or a fear of being ugly. I don't remember that. I think my issues were simply immaturity. I looked like a woman. I had all the equipment. Problem was, I was still a kid who thought jumping in the lake after Thanksgiving totally naked was a great idea.

This summer I found myself walking around the quays in my part of London. The unusually beautiful weather this year meant that I could walk around in a sundress and pretty sandals rather than pulling on some sensible but comfy outfit. Going along the quay one afternoon I noticed that I sat a little taller and greeted the men in the boatyard more confidently all the way around. I felt the breeze in between my thighs, a strong energy sliding down my spine and radiating through my hips. I suddenly wanted a pair of hands around my waist and to talk with someone who was as confident as I.

Within five minutes I had met a man fishing off the dock, and he and I were digging for worms. My sandals had been kicked off, and I was eyeing his cooler full of orange soda. So much for being a woman.

At the wedding this weekend I looked from the stranger, who at some point in time had jumped naked off my back dock, to Cristi in her white dress and veil. It may have been her day but I still needed an explanation.

"I don't know. You must've been at an audition or something. Heck if I know, I did it all the time without you."

"Cristi, I can't have random people jumping naked off my dock. Do you know how much trouble …?"

"Oh grow up," said the new wife.

Girls don't grow up in a consistent and straight line. Somewhere between the age we feel like, the age we actually are, and the age the world expects us to act, there is us. Our bodies seem much more confident than we are in them. And there are always women's voices coming from the shadows of the banks. Strong voices of sensual women promising all the treasures and secrets of femininity. Many girls instantly jump in, desperately trying to grow up way too fast and taste the mysteries which tempt men and women alike. Others hide under the dock, afraid to let go and swim into unknown waters.

More often than not there are young women who jump in naked just to be silly, only to realise later that nobody has a map of the lake. We get dangerously close to the sirens at times, and then we flee to take refuge underneath the dock. There are entire days spent back and forth, restless and trapped in one's foolishly mature body.

And there are days when we get closer to the bank than we can ever remember. And actually, we are quite comfortable just listening; we all know we are going to grow up someday, but none of us knows how to pass through the deep waters of the lake directly.

LETTER TO A
VERY WISE TEACHER

My Dear Teacher,

Today is our birthday. And like every year on this day, I am writing this to wish you many happy returns (although quite honestly I am not exactly sure what that phrase means. Returns from where exactly? But it is something we say often on this side of the pond so I'm bound to repeat the phrase as well). This year is a special birthday for us for three reasons.

1. I am now the age that you were when we first met. This supposedly means that I am a reasonable adult, although I honestly see very little proof of this.

2. This birthday now means, according to my arithmetic, I have known you for over half my lifetime.

3. You are, by my best calculations, forty-two years old today, which is the age we once assigned to Agamemnon while reading *The Iliad* together saying, "It's that age where nobody respects you because you're no longer young, but you're not old enough to be considered wise."

It is also an important birthday for me because I am now the age of Henry David Thoreau when he decided to build a cabin in the woods in order to learn to "live deliberately." At this age he already could see that life slips away fast, and unless you stop and truly learn how to breathe and live to the fullest, you just continue on, missing out on so much of what's in front of you, while wishing for tomorrow.

I used to want to escape to the woods. I think we all do at sometime or another, until the realities of what it would take to live a fully self-sufficient life sinks in. And for someone who will never be able to use an axe or pull water from a well, I've pretty much decided that it would be best to stay in a place where I can at least have access to running water, and a computer, and a power plug, and my DVD player, and my wheelchair, and … Thoreau was lucky. He didn't have cerebral palsy.

Living on the Thames over the past four years, however, has given me more of a sense of Walden Pond than our forefathers could have imagined when they fled to the new world. Here I have found myself in a community which has "gone Walden" as I watch my friends come out of their boats each morning, starting their day by chopping wood or varnishing their sterns, doing whatever needs to be done on that day to ensure that their homes stay above water. I have found myself, somehow, living with people who live deliberately as we share a co-dependent existence built on ensuring the community thrives and freedom is maintained. From the sounds of a hammer echoing across the dockyard, to the belly-filled "'Allo Love" I hear belted out each morning by the men jumping off their boat to go to work, I have discovered a life here that's full of questions, ideas, riddles, and verse which would rival the profundity found on a pond in Concord.

Of course, had I not been taught the skills I needed to be able to live deliberately, significant ideas or events would be lost on me completely. Life usually operates in different spheres between "meaning" and "living." The role of the artist, you once told me, is to bring these two spheres together into some sort of coexistence. My job is to take the seemingly haphazard events of life and rearrange them so that they mean something. This isn't that different from being a teacher except you bring order from the chaos in young people's minds. In many ways your brief is much more difficult.

So we must believe that life has order, something you instilled in me when I was still a teenager huddled over my desk attempting to finish an essay before the bell rang. It is an idea that is quickly becoming obsolete in our world as it seems easier to see that madness and futility rule the day. To me, that is the joy of living in the docklands of the

Thames. It is living side-by-side with these men on their boats, being a land dweller that loves and listens to them, and depending on their strength to accomplish tasks which are far beyond my capabilities, that allows me to see that life has meaning. Lessons from teachers such as yourself have taught me to believe in life. Living here I am allowed to see that meaning come into a tangible reality. Like all the best elements of life, belief in the significance of the individual must be first believed to be seen.

I think Thoreau got it very wrong. Meaning isn't found when one is in isolation, but in community. It is in living together, dealing with one another when you really don't want to be bothered, having lives that continually bump into each other and constantly create friction, refusing to walk away to a cabin in the woods, that we invest in each other and reap fruits from season after season of living together. To choose wilfully not to leave when things get difficult is the ultimate act of living deliberately. To realise that life is as fragile as a small boat on the Thames is to see the immense value of life. To be able to have both at the same time makes for the conditions to grow great ideas, create fantastic work, and cultivate a life remarkably well-lived.

I am loath to close. Attempting to link the past with the present is always too grand a task to muster in a single setting, as I'm sure you know being a history teacher yourself. I think having teachers such as you was how I began to live deliberately, an exercise I fully hope to continue to make a career of both at my desk and onstage. And yet as each birthday comes around I am struck by how it all gets quicker, seems to have ever increasing significance, and connects in the most dazzling of ways. Perhaps it is the realisation of the last that allows me to know that in an overpopulated high school on the north side of Chicago, fourteen years ago, you were helping to groom me for living this life on the Thames all along.

Happy birthday to us. May the next fourteen years be lived just as deliberately.